# SUPER FAST

# MONEY

## BECOME AN EXPERT
## & START MAKING MONEY TODAY!!

## 2019 Edition

properties of their respective owners. The author/publisher/reseller are not associated or affiliated with them in any way. Nor does the referred product, website, and company names sponsor, endorse, or approve this product.

**COMPENSATION DISCLOSURE:** Unless otherwise expressly stated, you should assume that the links contained in this book may be affiliate links and either the author/publisher/reseller will earn commission if you click on them and buy the product/service mentioned in this book. However, the author/publisher/reseller disclaim any liability that may result from your involvement with any such websites/products. You should perform due diligence before buying mentioned products or services.

This constitutes the entire license agreement. Any disputes or terms not discussed in this agreement are at the sole discretion of the publisher.

# Table of Contents

# Introduction

Are you looking for a **fast and easy way to make money online?**

If you're anything like me, you're probably fed up with the guides that tell you how you can generate instant profits online, only to be directed to ridiculous survey sites that pay pennies per hour.

You'd be lucky to be able to buy a cup of coffee with that nonsense!

Thankfully, there really are legitimate ways to make money online that don't take a lot of time, and in most cases, very little to no upfront investment. And that's what this special report is all about.

I'm going to save you a lot of time and trial-by-error by focusing on the **one instant income opportunity** that has not only worked for myself, but countless others and condensed everything into this short report.

# Instant

# Commission

# Networks

Have you ever heard of instant commission networks? These are marketplaces that will send you payment via PayPal **instantly** for every product you sell.

It's one of the most exciting opportunities online and one of the easiest, especially if you have any experience with affiliate marketing, or you already own a blog, website or mailing list.

Regardless, even if you're a complete beginner, you can still take advantage of these instant cash avenues just by following a few simple steps.

*Here's a quick breakdown of what you'll need to do:*

Create accounts at http://www.JVZoo.com
and http://www.WarriorPlus.com

These are two of the bigger instant-commission marketplaces so you'll want to focus on at least one of these.

*The idea behind them is a very simple one:*

- Choose products that you're interested in promoting.
- Apply to become an affiliate. Quite often you'll get accepted in minutes.
- Set up campaigns to promote the products.
- Earn money instantly, sent to your PayPal account!

Of course, there's more to each step and that's what we'll cover in this guide. Let's begin by setting up your accounts on both platforms.

The key is to fill out your profile completely, especially on Warrior Plus. You want to be attractive to those who are considering you as an affiliate, and while you won't have any stats to back up the fact you can sell products, a complete profile will make it easier to get that approval.

If you have a website, blog or social media presence, you'll want to include those links in your profile. It will help potential partners quickly approve you, and will demonstrate that you have at least some experience building accounts, profiles and have a bit of knowledge with online marketing.

If you don't have any of those things, no worries! You'll still be able to get approved for a variety of products on both JVZoo and Warrior Plus. However, you may be set on what is called "Delayed Commissions" for some of these products. This simply means that you won't receive commissions instantly but instead you'll be paid once the refund period is over.

Note that on JVZoo, you aren't given the opportunity to add a bio, social links or even your website however with WarriorPlus, you're able to create a complete profile page.

In the next chapter, I'll show you what kind of products to focus on so you can start making money quickly.

# Choosing The Best Products To Promote

Choosing the right products is key to maximizing your affiliate income. You not only want to focus on promoting products that are currently in demand, but you want to get on board during the **early phase of launches**.

*Why is this so important?*

People love launches. The hype, the buzz that's generated throughout the process, and the excitement from others who share the products and discuss what they love most about products all fuels the launch.

So, if you get in early, you'll be able to get the most out of your marketing efforts.  You want to be ready to promote as soon as the product goes live, beating out competing affiliates who are also promoting it.

Makes sense, right?

You'll always make more money promoting an active, and current launch than you would promoting evergreen products that have been on the market for a long time.

This means you'll want to pay attention to product launch calendars. This will tell you what upcoming launches are taking place so you can get prepared. This report is all about making money in 60 minutes or less, so you'll want to look at products launching today, if possible.

You can find out what launches are happening at http://www.MunchEye.com

Munch Eye has been around for years and is a valuable resource for anyone who wants to keep a pulse on upcoming launches, as well as a helpful calendar of events for vendors who may wish to launch their product on days where there's less activity.

You can find the launch calendar for JV Zoo here: https://muncheye.com/category/affiliate/jvzoo

And the calendar for Warrior Plus here: https://muncheye.com/category/affiliate/warrior-plus

And there's another reason to stay on top of upcoming launches: **Affiliate contests!**

Quite often, vendors will encourage affiliates to jump on board by offering additional incentives to promote their products. This usually includes cash prizes based on an affiliate leaderboard. Those who bring in the most sales will gain access to special bonuses.

Knowing what product launches are taking place will also help you maximize your income by **creating bonuses** that entice customers to purchase through your link rather than a competitor's. In the next chapter, I'll show you how to set one up so you can quickly maximize sales and skyrocket your income.

# Your Secret Weapon To Maximizing Your Income

It should come as no surprise that bonuses are what often separate regular affiliates from super affiliate marketers. After all, why would a customer purchase a product from you if someone else is offering a free add-on, upgrade or auxiliary component that adds value to their purchase?

People love getting something extra for nothing, so if you want to stand out while being able to build a successful career as a super affiliate, there's no easier way than by offering bonuses as part of your overall marketing campaign.

Here's the thing to keep in mind:
**Not all bonuses are created equal.**

If you've been around the affiliate marketing arena for any length of time, chances are you've already encountered an affiliate offering bonuses if you purchase through their link.

If you search for "bonus" in your inbox right now, you'll likely pull up dozens of emails from affiliates who are doing all they can to convince potential customers who purchase through their links.

But how many of those bonuses catch your attention?

An ordinary, run-of-the-mill bonus won't help you stand out.  Everyone is offering those.  If your bonus can be easily found online, it isn't going to help you convert clicks into sales.

In other words, your bonus needs to be as unique and special as you are. :)

*Here's the good news:*  Bonuses don't have to cost a lot of money or take a lot of time to create. Sure, if you're a content creator you've got the advantage of creating your own bonuses without having to pay a dime.  But if you suck at creating products, or just don't have time to do so, you can still join the leagues of super affiliates who utilize bonuses to double, even triple their income.

And no, I'm not going to send you over to Upwork.com where you can search for a qualified yet affordable freelance writer, designer or coder. You don't have to do any of that. Instead, I'm going to point you to the PLR membership where you can find thousands of bonuses for a small fee: InDigitalWorks.com

So, you now have your JVZoo and Warrior Plus accounts set up and ready to make you money. You've filled out your profile, added your PayPal email address and have signed up for InDigitalWorks so you have instant

access to gorgeous, in-demand bonus
packages.

Next up: Choosing products to promote!

# The Path to Success

I've already mentioned the importance of staying on top of upcoming product launches so you don't miss out on affiliate contests and other opportunities.  But what if there aren't any product launches happening today? Or this week? Or even this month? (though very unlikely).

No worries, there are thousands of products to choose from just between Warrior Plus and JV Zoo, not to mention other (non-instant commission) networks like www.ClickBank.com

So, here's how to start and what you want to pay close attention to when choosing your products:

First, make sure you've decided on a bonus package first because you're going to want to **align the bonus with a product in the same niche market.**
It doesn't make sense to offer a bonus that's not relevant to the products you intend to promote, right?

That's important, so always keep that in mind. Bonuses must align with your promoted products otherwise customers will end up confused, frustrated and well, they just won't buy from you again.

Since InDigitalWorks.com bonuses are focused on various niches, from online business and marketing to self help and fitness, if you plan to use their packages you'll want to search for products in similar niches.

When considering products you want to promote, you'll have to research the vendor as thoroughly as possible.

This includes:

**Looking over past product launches.** How well did their product do? How many sales did they generate? What kind of feedback did they receive?

With Warrior Plus, you'll see the average review score next to many products so pay attention to that when evaluating potential vendors.

You will want to take things a step further and check out their social media presence.

Follow them on twitter, friend them on Facebook and join any open groups they're in.

Do your best to evaluate their past launches and current products before you tie your name to it.

Your brand is your ticket to making money online and you never want to promote products that you haven't evaluated or vendor's you haven't conducted some sort of due diligence on.

When you've chosen a couple of products to promote, it's time to launch a marketing strategy that will get those PayPal payment notifications pouring in!

# Quick & Easy Marketing Strategies

How you launch a marketing campaign will depend on your available resources.

For example, if you have access to a mailing list, then the easiest way to jumpstart your affiliate marketing is to send out a broadcast to everyone on your list.

Or, if you have a presence on any of the social media sites with an avid following, you could post an update with affiliate links.

But what if you don't have any of these tools at your disposal? What do you do then?

**Give something away and build your lists!**

You can sign up for a free mailing list account at http://www.MailerLite.com which will let you grow a list up to 1,000 subscribers before you must upgrade to a paid account. This is more than enough room for you to begin building targeted lists before you have to fork out any money.

Once you set up a Mailer List account, you can use their drag and drop editor to create a quick lead capture page so you can begin to generate leads.

Your squeeze page should be very basic and include only the following:

**Opt-in form, above the fold.**

Strong headline that captures attention and prompts visitors to take action and enter their name and email address.

Highlight your freebie/giveaway. If possible, hire a graphic designer to create a 3D version of your product especially if you're giving away a report or eBook. You can find a cheap designer at http://www.Fiverr.com who can get it done quickly.

**Note about your give-away:** You want your incentive offer to be heavily focused on a specific niche market, so you'll want to decide what niche you're targeting first so you can build segmented lists for each market.

Consider your audience, the type of products you plan to promote, and what people are most likely interested in and then offer a giveaway that appeals to the majority of that market.

If you're stuck on what to give away, be sure to check out InDigitalWorks where you'll be able to instantly snag dozens of done-for-you lead magnets that include everything you need to start growing targeted lists.

This includes:

**Squeeze page:** Professionally designed, responsive templates that make it drop dead easy to start capturing leads. Just swap the opt-in form for your own.

**Polished Reports:** These short reports (20-25 pages) are all written by professionals with hands-on experience with the topics they cover.

They're focused on in-demand markets and provide how-to style instructions so you're able to provide clear value to subscribers who are interested in learning more about a variety of hot topics.

**7-Day Follow Up Series:** You'll want to plug these autoresponder sequences into your mailing list account so you can set your communication and list growth on autopilot. These autoresponder messages are geared towards nurturing a relationship with your target audience which will make it easy for you to sell more products and grow a brand of your own.

InDigitalWorks is one of the only sites to provide such fully loaded lead magnet packages, so if you're looking to shortcut the steps involved in building profitable mailing lists, this resource will quickly become your secret list building weapon.

When your squeeze page is up, your giveaway is set to go out on autopilot the minute a subscriber joins your list, and you have a couple of products ready to promote, it's time to drive targeted traffic to your page.

In the final chapter of this special report I'll show you how to launch your campaign quickly.

We have 60 minutes, right? Let's make it count!

# High Speed Traffic Triggers

While you could spend some time creating social marketing campaigns such as Facebook boosted posts or promotional tweets, if you're looking to jumpstart your affiliate campaigns quickly, and at very little cost, you'll want to choose one of the traffic triggers below.

## #1: Free Community Networks

You could start by joining relevant Facebook groups, participating in open discussions and driving traffic to your squeeze page from those who check out your Facebook account and choose to follow (or friend) you. And speaking of which, don't forget to post a link to your squeeze page as a new post on your Facebook profile.

Also, don't overlook **Q&A networks** as viable traffic channels. Answer common questions within your niche market on websites like: Quora, Blurt it, and Fun Advice.

**Tip:** Linking to blog posts in your answers will get traffic to your site quickly and showcase your business as a thought leader in your industry. So, post a brief answer on the community site itself and then link to one of your own blog posts in order to drive in traffic.

## #2: Forums

While forums aren't nearly as popular as they used to be, there are still a few that provide a fantastic source of steady traffic.

If you're in the Internet Marketing or Make Money Online (MMO) niche, join the WarriorForum.com,

DigitalPoint.com, https://www.wickedfire.com/ and http://www.v7n.com/forums/

You may also want to explore https://growthhackers.com/posts and https://growth.org/discuss

While it's an old-school approach, it still works.  You can add a link to your squeeze page in your forum signature which is seen each time you post. When it comes to forums like the Warrior Forum, consider joining the "War Room" and sharing something valuable (like one of the lead magnet reports from InDigitalWorks) in order to quickly drive traffic to your page.

Also, drop by Linkedin Groups at

https://www.linkedin.com/groups/ to

search for active discussions in your niche

as well exploring subreddits where you can

answer questions from within your niche.

You can begin your search here:

https://www.reddit.com/


**#3: Blog Commenting**

When it comes to siphoning traffic from one

blog to another, there are a few things to

keep in mind.  First, you'll want to set up a

blog of your own. It doesn't have to be

fancy at all, just install Wordpress, choose a

professional theme from the free

marketplace, include a link to your squeeze

page (or better yet, incorporate the opt-in code directly into your post).

That way when you comment on authority blogs and people see the link back to your site, when people choose to visit your website they aren't seeing an empty page.

Give them enough content to satisfy their interest and direct them to your squeeze page.

This might sound like a bit of work, but it's well worth the effort. Having a centralized landing page (via your blog) to direct people to will make your job a lot easier.

Remember, everything you do should be in alignment with your brand, so even if you choose to save time and money by repurposing content, you'll still want to modify it enough so that it's your own.

When commenting on blogs with the intention of redirecting traffic to your own website, make sure that you're providing value in exchange. You never want to be a link drop drive-by kind of user.

Instead, answer questions thoughtfully, extend the conversation to include additional tools, resources, or provide an alternative perspective on a current topic. The more authoritative you sound, the easier it will be to drive traffic from their blog to yours. Plus, you'll likely end up on the radar of established bloggers which may open the possibility for future networking opportunities!

## #4: Pin It and They Will Come

Pinterest is a great channel for connecting with your target audience quickly, and free.  You'll want to hire a graphic designer to create an eye-catching graphic that drives people to your squeeze page.

**Tip:** Save money by signing up for a free account at http://www.Canva.com where you can easily create your own Pinterest and other marketing graphics at no cost, and with no graphic design experience needed.

The key with sites like Pinterest is to drive traffic to a landing page rather than directly to a vendor via your affiliate link. Warm up your traffic by leading them to a valuable resource and capture their information so you can follow up later on.

# Final Words

I hope that this special report helps you get on the path towards ongoing success in affiliate marketing.  The key is to stay consistent.  Look for ways to drive traffic to your squeeze pages, power up your mailing list account with in-demand freebies, useful content and autoresponders that nurture engagement.

Keep tabs on upcoming product launches,

keeping in mind that heavy promotions on the first and last day of a launch will typically yield the best results.

In fact, over 25% of all sales are usually made on day one with the remainder taking place on the final day.

Always be on the lookout for ways to spread your squeeze page links around. Share them on every social media platform you can, incorporate them into blog posts, and try to be as active on external sites as you are on your own.

Utilize guest blogging, blog commenting and forum marketing to your advantage. Remember, the more active you are across multiple platforms, the more exposure you'll receive.

Affiliate marketing is a numbers game. You want to try as many different things as possible until you find what works for you.

Your primary focus should always be on continuing to **build your lists**. The more segmented, targeted and active your lists are, the more money you'll make.

We've covered a lot in the last 60 minutes or so! I hope that you have a clear objective in mind and that you now take action to make it happen. You can do this!

To your success!